Taste of City Food and Place Marketing Conference 2018
Programme and Abstracts Book

Compiled by
Ibrahim Sirkeci & Evinç Doğan

TRANSNATIONAL PRESS LONDON
2018

Taste of City Food and Place Marketing Conference 2018 - Programme and Abstracts Book

Compiled by Ibrahim Sirkeci & Evinç Doğan

Copyright © 2018 by Transnational Press London

All rights reserved.

First Published in 2018 by TRANSNATIONAL PRESS LONDON in the United Kingdom, 12 Ridgeway Gardens, London, N6 5XR, UK.

www.tplondon.com

Paperback

ISBN: 978-1-910781-89-0

Conference website: tastecity.net

CONTENT: SESSIONS AND TIMETABLE

**Taste of City Food and Place Marketing
Conference 2018 - Programme and
Abstracts Book**
4th– 5th October 2018
Akdeniz University, Antalya, Turkey

Welcome to the TOC 2018

We're pleased to welcome you to Akdeniz
University, Antalya in October for the Taste
of City: Food and Place Marketing
Conference 2018, which is hosted by Akdeniz
University Tourism Research, Development
and Application Centre (TAGUM) on 4-5
October 2018.

The TOC 2018 Antalya is an international
peer-reviewed academic research conference
with a focus on understanding the dynamics
and role of food play in place marketing and
branding. This unique event aims to bring
together researchers, scholars and
practitioners to explore the ways in which
food and places are marketed in an
interconnected fashion.

Invited Speakers in this year's conference
include Prof Zafer Yenal from Bogazici

University, Istanbul, Prof Pieter Terhorst from the University of Amsterdam and Prof Ibrahim Sirkeci from Regent's University London.

The TOC 2018 will bring different case studies around the world in focus. The key thematic areas are diverse with a multidisciplinary approach revolving around marketing, tourism, gastronomy and culture. The sub-thematic areas are as follows, in which the submission of proposals is usually encouraged although we are open for any other relevant topic: Marketing including Place marketing and branding, Food and drinks marketing, Food in place branding, Diaspora marketing, Consumer behaviour, International marketing, Cross cultural marketing; Tourism including Food tourism and destination branding, Food as touristic product in place marketing, Food and sustainable tourism, Food and alternative tourism, Food and health tourism, Food festivals and event marketing; Gastronomy including Molecular gastronomy and place marketing, Food, health and place marketing, Slow Food - Slow Cities, Creative cities of gastronomy, Gastronomic experience – Taste hunts; Culture including Transnational food, Religion and food: Halal and Kosher, Heritage food, Diasporas and exporting heritage taste, Food crossing borders, Food mobility: Tacos to Doner, Feta to Curry, and Diasporas, foods, places.

Throughout the program of the Conference you will find various key thematic areas are covered in presentations by academics and researchers from around the world including Australia, Israel, the Netherlands, Turkey and the UK.

Here we should also make an announcement from next year onwards, the scope of the conference will be expanded and the series will be renamed as Transnational Marketing Conference. We will keep the food and place marketing as one of the key streams in the new format.

Hope to see you join us in the next conference.

Warm regards,

Evinç Doğan and Ibrahim Sirkeci

On behalf of The Taste of City Conference Committee

Supporting Organisations

- Akdeniz University Tourism Research, Development and Application Centre (TAGUM)

- Akdeniz University Tourism Faculty

  http://turizm.akdeniz.edu.tr/en

- Regent's University London, Centre for Transnational Business and Management (RCTBM)

  https://www.regents.ac.uk/rcts

- Transnational Marketing Journal (TMJ)

  https://www.transnationalmarket.com/

- Advances in Hospitality and Tourism Research (AHTR)

  http://www.ahtrjournal.org/

Main Speakers:

Zafer Yenal

Zafer Yenal is a professor of sociology at Boğaziçi University. His research interests include the sociology of consumption, food studies, rural sociology, and historical sociology. His most recent book, Bildiğimiz Tarımın Sonu (The End of Agriculture as We Know It) (with Çağlar Keyder, published by Iletişim Yayinlari, 2013), focuses on agricultural transformations in Turkey since the 1980s. His latest article, "Culinary Work at the Crossroads in Istanbul" (co-authored with Michael Kubiena), was published in *Gastronomica* (vol. 16, n. 1) in 2016. He is currently a member of the editorial boards of *New Perspectives on Turkey* and *Gastronomica: The Journal of Critical Food Studies*.

Pieter Terhorst

Pieter Terhorst is an emeritus ass. Professor at the University of Amsterdam (Department of Geography, Planning and International development Studies). He specialized in economic geography, variety of capitalism, tourism cities, clusters, and rescaling of state spaces. He is co-editor (with Robert Kloosterman and Virginie Mamadouh) of the handbook "Geographies of Globalization" to be published by Edward Elgar.

Ibrahim Sirkeci

Ibrahim Sirkeci is Professor of Transnational Studies & Marketing and Director of Centre for Transnational Business and Management (RCTBM) at Regent's University London. Ibrahim Sirkeci has a Ph.D. in Geography (University of Sheffield), BA in Political Science and Public Administration (Bilkent University) and PG Certificate in Higher Education (University College London). Professor Sirkeci has coined the term "transnational mobile consumers" and also known for his extensive work on insecurity and human mobility. He is editor of several journals including *Transnational Marketing Journal*, *Remittances Review* and *Migration Letters*. His books include *Turkey's Syrians: Today and Tomorrow* (2017, Transnational Press London), *Transnational Marketing and Transnational Consumers* (2013, Springer), and *Migration and Remittances during the Global Financial Crisis and Beyond* (2012, World Bank.

ORGANISING TEAM

Conference Chairs

- ❖ Beykan Çizel, Akdeniz University, Turkey
- ❖ Ibrahim Sirkeci, Regent's University London, UK

Conference Organizing Committee

- ❖ Ebru İçigen, Akdeniz University, Turkey
- ❖ Osman Çalışkan, Akdeniz University, Turkey
- ❖ Emre İpekçi Çetin, Akdeniz University, Turkey
- ❖ Hilal Erkuş Öztürk, Akdeniz University, Turkey
- ❖ Koray Çetin, Akdeniz University, Turkey
- ❖ Evinç Doğan, Akdeniz University, Turkey
- ❖ Edina Ajanovic, Akdeniz University, Turkey
- ❖ Nevin Karabıyık Yerden, Marmara University, Turkey
- ❖ Ece Ömüriş, Akdeniz University, Turkey
- ❖ Dilek Hale Aybar, Akdeniz University, Turkey
- ❖ Adem Arman, Akdeniz University, Turkey

- ❖ Zeynep Karsavuran, Akdeniz University, Turkey
- ❖ Nilgün Güneş, Akdeniz University, Turkey
- ❖ Onur Selçuk, Akdeniz University, Turkey

Conference Scientific Advisory Committee:

- ❖ Per-Olof Berg, Stockholm University, Sweden
- ❖ Osman Çalışkan, Akdeniz University, Turkey
- ❖ Koray Çetin, Akdeniz University, Turkey
- ❖ Beykan Çizel, Akdeniz University, Turkey
- ❖ Jeffrey H. Cohen, Ohio State University, US
- ❖ Paolo Corvo, University of Gastronomic Sciences, Italy
- ❖ John Dawson, University of Edinburgh Business School, UK
- ❖ Evinç Doğan, Akdeniz University, Turkey
- ❖ Yakın Ekin, Akdeniz University, Turkey
- ❖ C. Michael Hall, University of Canterbury, New Zealand
- ❖ Ebru İçigen, Akdeniz University, Turkey
- ❖ Emre İpekçi Çetin, Akdeniz University, Turkey
- ❖ Metin Kozak, Dokuz Eylül University, Turkey

- ❖ Nazmi Kozak, Anadolu University, Turkey
- ❖ Robert D. Lemon, University of Heidelberg, Germany
- ❖ Ludovica Leone, University of Bologna Business School, Italy
- ❖ Jonathan Liu, Regent's University London, UK
- ❖ Eduardo Oliveira, Swiss Federal Research Institute WSL, Switzerland
- ❖ Maktoba Omar, Coventry University, UK.
- ❖ Ece Ömüriş, Akdeniz University, Turkey
- ❖ Marc Oliver Opresnik, Lübeck University of Applied Sciences, Germany
- ❖ Bahattin Özdemir, Akdeniz University, Turkey
- ❖ Hilal Erkuş Öztürk, Akdeniz University, Turkey
- ❖ Goran Petkovic, University of Belgrade, Serbia
- ❖ Jeffrey M. Pilcher, University of Toronto Scarborough, Canada
- ❖ Stefan Rohdewald, Historisches Institut, Justus-Liebig-Universität, Germany
- ❖ Paulette Schuster, The Open University of Israel, Hebrew University of Jerusalem
- ❖ Nurşah Şengül, Akdeniz University, Turkey

- ❖ Omar Al Serhan, Higher Colleges of Technology, Abu Dhabi, UAE
- ❖ Ibrahim Sirkeci, Regent's University London, UK
- ❖ Aleksandra Stupar, University of Belgrade, Serbia
- ❖ Zafer Yenal, Department of Sociology, Bogazici University, Turkey
- ❖ Nevin Karabıyık Yerden, Marmara University, Turkey

Supporting Organisations
- ❖ Akdeniz University Tourism Research, Development and Application Centre (TAGUM), Antalya, Turkey
- ❖ Akdeniz University Tourism Faculty, Antalya, Turkey
- ❖ Regent's University Centre for Transnational Studies, UK
- ❖ Transnational Marketing Journal, UK
- ❖ Advances in Hospitality and Tourism Research, Turkey

Conference Venue: Tourism Facutly of Akdeniz University, Antalya, Turkey

About Transportation

From Antalya International Airport to Akdeniz University main campus;

There are two options for participants who will come by plane;.

- By taxi: it is far approximetly 17 km and it takes 15 or 20 minutes. Its fee for this distance is between 60-70 TL. You may book a taxi on web page (http://www.antalyaairporttaxi.net/iletisim.php) or by whats up message: 0090 539 488 1616)

- By City Bus: it is red and goes to the entrance of University main campus in 40 minutes. You can get in it in front of the Antalya Airport Domestic Terminal. One way ticket's price is 5,2 TL.

About Accommodation

First option is Guest House of Akdeniz University and it;

- includes breakfast.

- is in the main campus and far to the Tourism Faculty by walking is only 5 minutes.

- is far to the sea only 850m.

- has private pool (free) and massage service (paid).

- has wi-fi internet.

- http://sks.akdeniz.edu.tr/resim-galerisi

- Phone number is: 0090 242 310 2003

Note: Limited rooms are booked for participants. If you would like to stay there, please make your reservation as soon as possible.

Few other nearest hotels which you would prefer:

Rixos Downtown Antalya: http://downtownantalya.rixos.com/

Özkaymak Falez Hotel: http://falez.ozkaymakhotels.com.tr/

Grida City Hotel Antalya: http://www.gridacity.com/

Hotel Su and Aqualand: http://hotel-su.antalyahotel.org/en/

OPENNING SESSION &
WELCOMING SPEECHES

Conference Venue: Akdeniz University,
Tourism Faculty - Nuri Özaltın
Conference Hall

4.10.2018 - THURSDAY

Registration Desk Opens	**10:30**
Pre-Conference Seminar	**11:00-12:00**
Research in Germany - Franziska Trepke (Director of DAAD - Ankara) *Room: Nuri Özaltın Conference Hall*	
Exhibition tour: Research in Germany *Foyer Area*	**12:00**

Opening & Plenary Session:	13:30-13:45

Welcoming speech:

Prof Beykan Çizel, Akdeniz University (Dean of Tourism Faculty)

Keynote speeches:	13:45-15:45

Prof Pieter Terhorst, University of Amsterdam, Netherlands
Prof Zafer Yenal, Bogazici University, Turkey
Prof Ibrahim Sirkeci, Regent's University London, United Kingdom

RESTAURANTS AND THE CITY
Pieter Terhorst

Abstract
My keynote speech is about restaurants and the city, which is made up of three sections. In the first section, I discuss, in general terms, the effects of the concentration of restaurants in cities on the functioning of the restaurant industry. In the second section, I discuss what leading sociologists (Mennell, Warde, Ritzer, Bourdieu, and Johnston & Baumann) have to say on changes in food consumption in Europe and the US. One main conclusion is that

traditional ways of distinction by means of food consumption have given way to omnivorousness, which is particularly an urban phenomenon. In the third section, I discuss how quality uncertainty in urban fields of restaurants is reduced. Food and drinks served in restaurants, the quality of which cannot be objectively determined. Based on Bourdieu's theory of the production of symbolic goods, I argue that quality is the result of a consensus among key actors in the field of restaurants: chefs, cooks, restaurateurs, culinary journalists, and consumers. Quality standards are set by past careers of restaurateurs, master-apprentice relations, job hopping of chefs and cooks, monitoring, relations with media, and strategies of distinction by local consumers (not tourists). The process of setting quality standards is partly local, partly national, and partly global.

***

CITY'S ANEW TASTE FOR AGRICULTURE

Zafer Yenal

Abstract

In this keynote speech I explore the nature of interactions between the urban and the rural in terms of food consumption and production patterns in the last several decades. We are witnessing "a rediscovery of agriculture" by the urban middle-classes, as exemplified by the rising popularity of urban farming activities in major cities across the world and by the growing number of urban dwellers who question the qualities and standards of food with respect to human health, environmental sustainability and social welfare. New fads and fashions with strong emphasis on local and natural qualities of food have found wider currency not only among consumers but also among prominent chefs, food writers and even major food companies. Whether and how do all these transform the existing interactions between the city and the countryside? What are the limitations and potentialities of these developments for achieving a better food world? I will try to develop responses to these questions by focusing on the mutual dynamics of urban dwellers' food preferences, tastes, and concerns and new agrarian patterns in contemporary Turkey.

***

PASSPORT SALE OR SELLING A COUNTRY: CITIZENSHIP OFFERS TO ELITE CUSTOMERS

Ibrahim Sirkeci

Abstract

Today in my keynote address, I would like to draw attention to a relatively new and growing area of place marketing: citizenship and residency sales. Many large and small states introduced various programmes and schemes to attract foreign investors. However, given the rising concerns and widespread human insecurity risks, super rich of the developing world emerged as a target segment for a special niche product. In this paper, the market is explored and the key attributes of the products offered are examined. It is still unclear whether the push for this category of products came from supply side or demand side. Some suppliers (e.g. large countries attracting sizeable immigration) price their products very highly and yet remain competitive whereas many small states offer citizenship or residency at bargain prices. The target segment is economically highly wealthy families and individuals from developing countries and particularly from China. The product attributes include one essential service elements (i.e. visa free travel access to many countries) along with some others (e.g. tax avoidance –or management- opportunities and real investment opportunities). Status or prestige also comes with the fact that holding a second passport, holding a passport of a particular country, and being able to travel to many countries without visa.

***

Coffee Break	15:45-16:00

SESSION 1 – Food Attributes Crossing Borders

Room: Nuri Özaltın Conference Hall	**16:00**
	-
Chair: Ibrahim Sirkeci	**17:45**

Paulette Schuster - FROM AUSTERITY TO ABUNDANCE: THE EVOLUTION OF ISRAELI FOOD, 1950'S-2000'S

Isami Omori - THE UNESCO RECOGNITION REINFORCED KYOTO BRAND IN FOOD THROUGH JAPANESE NEWSPAPERS

Bahattin Özdemir, Zeynep Karsavuran, Gökhan Yılmaz - HEDONISM AND FOOD ATTRIBUTES WHEN CONSUMING STREET FOODS: A PILOT STUDY

Doğuş Kılıçarslan, Özge Kocabulut - ANCIENT JUJUBE (ZIZYPHUS) FESTIVAL IN ANTALYA

FROM AUSTERITY TO ABUNDANCE: THE EVOLUTION OF ISRAELI FOOD, 1950'S-2000'S

Paulette Schuster

Abstract

From 1949 to 1959, the nascent state of Israel was under a regime of austerity (known as Tzena in Hebrew), during which rationing was instituted. At the outset, rationing only encompassed basic staple foods such as oil, sugar and margarine but was later expanded to include other foodstuffs, furniture and footwear. Each month, each person would receive food coupons and each family was allotted a given amount of foodstuffs. The diet was modelled after the United Kingdom which also had a regime of rationing during World War II.

During this time due to the severe calorie restrictions and limited food resources, austerity menus and recipes were published in the local newspapers and magazines to encourage citizens, especially women, to be creative in the kitchen and to stretch what little ingredients they had and make due. Fast-forward 69 years since the end of these black years in Israeli history to today. Israel is thriving economically and in the culinary scene.

I am interested in exploring how these women actually made due during Tzena? How did they stretch and multiply their food provisions? How did this austerity period shape their collective psyche? Did they transmit the fear of not having enough to their children? If so, how did that attitude shape today's consumer patterns? Did it change how food is currently viewed and marketed? Which foodstuffs were promoted then and now? And in which channels?

Objectives

The main objective is to compare two period of Israeli history: Austerity and recovery and how Israeli food has evolved.

Methods

Twenty interviews will be conducted in Israel in total. Ten will be conducted with Israelis who lived during Tzena and ten with Israelis of today. They will be carried out in various cities in Israel. Participant observation will also take place, as well as, a review of the existing literature.

Preliminary Results

It is too early to form any definitive conclusions but it seems that Israelis who endured Tzena had a deeply embedded fear of running out of food. This fear was transferred to their descendents who do not know what it means to go hungry. For them, this period of austerity is a part of history. For them, abundance is all they know.

***

THE UNESCO RECOGNITION REINFORCED KYOTO BRAND IN FOOD THROUGH JAPANESE NEWSPAPERS

Isami Omori

Abstract

The aim of this research is to discuss what influence has the nominating Japanese food (Washoku) for inscription on UNESCO's list of Intangible Cultural Heritage in 2013 exerted on the image of place associated with Japanese food through newspapers in Japan. The ratings of 47 place names in Japan and 50 related words in the Japanese newspapers articles containing the three words for Japanese food, called nihonshoku, nihonryori and washoku in Japanese were evaluated. This research was implemented in 3 Japanese nation-wide newspapers over 8 years period, 2009-2016. The appearance ratio of each place name and keyword in the articles compared the ratio of change before and after the nomination. The results showed that appearance of place name in these articles was limited geographically. More than 30% of the total appearance of place names is composed of Tokyo, Osaka and Kyoto, and furthermore, the growth ratio of appearance of Kyoto was more than 50% during 2009 and 2016, higher than that of Tokyo and Osaka. The highest appearance ratio of keyword was "taste", and additionally, "culture", "heritage", "world", "abroad", "local" and "tradition" had high appearance ratio after the nomination. The results suggest that UNESCO recognition linked the words which are concerned with place and memory to Japanese food. As a result, Kyoto created further added value thorough the combination of historical image and tasty image by the UNESCO nomination, and enhanced the brand strength of Kyoto's food through these articles.

***

HEDONISM AND FOOD ATTRIBUTES WHEN CONSUMING STREET FOODS: A PILOT STUDY

Bahattin Özdemir, Zeynep Karsavuran, Gökhan Yılmaz

Abstract

This study aims to explore the antecedents of streets foods consumption. Attributes of street foods and perception of hedonism are tested as two potent variables to predict intentions to consume street foods. Data is composed of 71 surveys collected from street food consumers. The results of the study revealed that food attributes are important to predict both street foods consumption and perception of hedonism. However, when hedonism is added to the hierarchical regression analysis, food attributes is fully mediated by hedonism, showing the prevalence of hedonic consumption as the primary antecedent of street foods patronage. Since intentions to consume street foods have not been investigated in detail so far, these study findings are potent to stimulate new research questions and theoretical discussions.

***

ANCIENT JUJUBE (ZIZYPHUS) FESTIVAL IN ANTALYA

Doğuş Kılıçarslan, Özge Kocabulut

Abstract

In this research, it was aimed to evaluate Antique Jujube Festival which is a forgotten event among the culinary events held in Antalya. In addition, in this study, various information about the juniper tree which led to the festival organized in the antique age was given and the effect of the food and beverage festivals on the tourism industry was evaluated. Finally, it was concluded with suggestions that would contribute to the development of the destination in terms of tourism festival.

Taste of City Conference Reception	**17:45-19:00**

Following the opening keynote speeches, participants of the Taste of City: Food and Place Marketing Conference 2018 are invited to a drinks reception by Akdeniz University Tourism Research, Development and Application Centre (TAGUM) on 4 October 2018.

5.10.2018 – FRIDAY

Registration Desk Opens - 09:30

SESSION 2 – Diasporas, Foods, Places

Room: Nuri Özaltın Conference Hall	09:45 -
Chair: Yıldırım Yılmaz	11:15

Jukhruf Binth Junaid - DIASPORA BAZAAR IN OCCIDENTAL SYDNEY

Özge Çopuroğlu - THE ROLE OF THE FOOD IN NATIONAL IDENTITY IN THE MIDDLE EAST: SOCIAL AND POLITICAL ASPECTS OF "HUMMUS WARS".

Hossain Mohammed - FORMATION OF TASTE IN VIRTUAL MARKETPLACE: A POST-MODERNIST PERSPECTIVE

Ibrahim Sirkeci, Fatma Zeren - FULL ENGLISH BREAKFAST WITH SPICY TURKISH SAUSAGE

THE ROLE OF THE FOOD IN NATIONAL IDENTITY IN THE MIDDLE EAST: SOCIAL AND POLITICAL ASPECTS OF "HUMMUS WARS".

Özge Çopuroğlu

Abstract

Food is an essential part of our everyday lives and it is significantly important for international politics as for the national identities. The future of food is widely discussed in political and social sciences in the contexts of the food security, health, international marketing and cultural identities.

This study aims to explore the connection between food and nationalism and it argues that food plays a central role in performing the nation's culture and expresses the idea of the nation through portraying material and spiritual aspects of the national identity.

We will basically seek to answer the following questions: 1) How food is used to perform and symbolize the nation by defining national identity through food? 2) Hummus' culturally complicated and obscure roots have conspired to create a tension over the dish's actual origin, with several countries laying claim to it. Can we use the debate over its origins as a filter for the current conflict?

It is a fact that, the chickpeas and sesame oil which are the basic ingredients of hummus had been widely cultivated in the Middle East and used as food by several groups, i.e. Arabs, Turks, Armenians and Jews. It is another fact that before the 20th Century there were no such national boundaries in the Region and a question about possessing the hummus by a certain group was meaningless. But today, it is just the time for a possible struggle towards possessing hummus by a Middle Eastern country as an important food in its national cuisine.

Our case study of "hummus wars" in the Middle East is expected to demonstrate how the public participates actively in creating and sustaining national identity, whether it is originally Lebanese, Syrian, Palestinian or Israeli.

Departing from Atsuko Ichijo's and Ronal Renta's points of view on the matter of national identity and food, we'll try to re-open to discussion if the international organizations plays the role of the mediator in such conflicts or contrarily, do they promote nationalism and national identity.

***

DIASPORA BAZAAR IN OCCIDENTAL SYDNEY
Jukhruf Binth Junaid

Abstract

Lakemba, generally renowned as a Halal food hub for Sydney-siders transforms to a mystic Bazaar in an occidental setting during the month of Ramadan. It is astonishing to find how the ethnic diaspora has embodied this Inner West suburb of Sydney into a cultural and foodie place with a variety of Middle Eastern cuisines. This research collated through in-depth interviews indicates that the social development of diaspora is the navigating factor contributing to food and place marketing for Lakemba. Ramadan in Lakemba marks a seasonal occasion for families to gather in an interactive platform and enjoy safe crowd practice. Gastronomy takes a complete new dimension as the Middle Eastern cuisine transfigures into street food to suit the Australian taste bud.

Not only is it food that attracts the humming crowd but it is also the eclectic culture of late night celebrations, meeting and mingling of people from diverse backgrounds coming to enjoy the safe crowd practice that shapes this developing night-life in Lakemba, Sydney.

***

FORMATION OF TASTE IN VIRTUAL MARKETPLACE: A POST-MODERNIST PERSPECTIVE

Hossain Mohammed

Abstract

Foodies in the Post-modernist era devote a great deal of their time surfing the Virtual Marketplace in search of taste-worthy items. Consumer perception of taste, especially of food from cultures other than their own is increasingly embedded in this virtual space. In the virtual zone, a foodie's perception of a cuisine becomes that of an art, an authentic piece, and a story worth telling. The abundance in online reviews, criticism and opinions enable a pre-purchase selection of items becoming a risk worth taking for numerous individuals. This paper applies Discourse Analysis to explore how foodies select cuisines from exclusive cultures through the use of communications and media. Online reviews are an integral and influential precedent which enable the amass of a web centric virtual marketplace. This platform of storytelling as well as sharing a personal experience influence customer's pre-purchase decision matrix further propagating the Virtual Marketplace of Food.

***

FULL ENGLISH BREAKFAST WITH SPICY TURKISH SAUSAGE

Ibrahim Sirkeci, Fatma Zeren

Abstract

This study presents an inquiry for the relationship between the market entry modes of diaspora entrepreneurs with social capital. Putnam (1993) refers to the concept of social capital as connections within and between social networks and the value that an individual gets from the social network. Ionescu (2007, p.8) defines diasporas as: "members of ethnic and national communities, who have left, but maintain links with, their homelands". The links minimizes the effects of border and geography. This transnational nature of diaspora entrepreneurship enables to transfer innovation and knowledge from the host country to the home country (Newland and Tanaka, 2010). So in this study the effects of social capital on diasporas entrepreneurship examined from three perspectives: network of origin (ethnic, national), network of destination, and network of industry (Drori et al., 2009).

Networks of origin frequently play a key role in the selection of destination, as well as in getting used to live in this new neighborhood. Networks of destination are building social capital in the form of interaction and trust. Industry networks, providing access to critical resources, including jobs, knowledge, and customers.

As a result of the diaspora / immigrant initiatives, it appears that many developed economies have gained a more cosmopolitan outlook, especially in the larger cities. This is now reflected not only in obvious items such as Coca Cola, McDonalds, CNN and Sneakers but also in an expanding product range such as Turk Cola, McDoner, Aljazeera and colorful headscarf (Rath, 2006). As a consequence of this effect, there is a large product range of Turkish products in London. The sample of this study consists of Turkish entrepreneurs who have been marketing Pınar brand sausage in London. A qualitative type of research with interpretative approach will conduct. Data will collect through interview with entrepreneurs.

Coffee Break	11:15-11:30

SESSION 3 – Coffee and Coffee Shops as Cultural Tourism Products

Room: Nuri Özaltın Conference Hall	11:30 -
Chair: Evinç Doğan	13:00

Erhan Akarçay - NEW WAVE OF COFFEE SHOPS IN ESKISEHIR: CHANGING COFFEE CULTURE

Evren Doğan, Evinç Doğan, Edina Ajanovic - MEMORY, SPACE & REPRESENTATION: TRANSFORMING IMAGE OF KAHVEHANES AND KAFANAS IN LEISURE CONSUMPTION

Nevin Karabıyık Yerden, İlknur Ergün Tuncay - "TURKISH COFFEE" AS A CULTURAL PRODUCT AND COMPETITIVE ANALYSIS FOR TURKISH COFFEE

Defne Karaosmanoglu - FOODSCAPES AND PLACE-MAKING: QUESTIONS OF METHODOLOGY

NEW WAVE OF COFFEE SHOPS IN ESKISEHIR: CHANGING COFFEE CULTURE

Erhan Akarçay

Abstract

In this paper, I will analyse local and independent coffee shops, their narratives comprising how they market various kinds of coffee beans, their ways of roasting, brewing, interior designs in relation to changing coffee culture in Turkey. I will focus on a middle-sized city Eskisehir in central Anatolia, where it is a globalizing and "Europeanizing" city, over 25 local coffee shops are opened in the last decade. Semi-structured interviews are made with coffee shop owners and their narratives are analysed in order to understand how they contribute in changing coffee culture.

Coffee culture in Turkey, particularly in big cities, is changing rapidly. As traditional coffee (Turkish coffee) consumption is well known and widely accepted drinking pattern in Turkey, consecutively instant coffee, global coffee chains (Starbucks, Gloria Jeans) are introduced to the society. Articulation of national economy with the global economy, urbanization and gentrification processes, rising numbers of shopping malls, consumer culture are the main reasons why coffee culture in relation to consumer culture has become prevalent in the society. In the last decade third wave coffee shops started to be opened.

In Eskisehir, local and independent coffee shops attempt to market their unique narratives. They narrate their coffee beans history, how their trade relations are fair. Most of these shops' interior design resemble each other in a given setting like industrial pipes, bicycles, light bulbs, menus on the blackboard written with chalks etc. What they serve in their menu also determined by food fads in Turkey. Most of the local coffee shops, global and local chains are mostly busy since coffee shops are becoming alternative to pubs as changing public sphere places and as political climate transforms society to a more conservative one.

***

MEMORY, SPACE & REPRESENTATION: TRANSFORMING IMAGE OF KAHVEHANES AND KAFANAS IN LEISURE CONSUMPTION

Evren Doğan, Evinç Doğan, Edina Ajanovic

Abstract

The similarities between the Kafanas in Belgrade and the Kahvehanes in Istanbul are notable demonstrating that the kahvehane concept introduced by the Ottomans had been highly adopted by the Belgradians. Originating as part of the Ottoman Culture, in today's modern world both kahvehanes and kafanas still exist as part of the daily life. In two different countries, Turkey and Serbia, they still continue to serve for the same purpose despite small differences. In this framework, the aim of the study is to explore the symbolic meanings behind transforming the image of kahvehanes located in Istanbul and kafanas in Belgrade throughout the history. The conceptual framework defines the city as a place of memory, while the contextual framework delves into meanings to identify common and contrasting themes between the old and contemporary cities. In this respect, memory is addressed as an important part of the cultural heritage to be passed to the next generations in consideration with the dynamism and rapid change of cities. Accordingly, the different social, political and economic functions of these places are analyzed in order to better understand their role in highlighting the framework of urban space and conceptions of gender in the Ottoman world while representing both simple and complex realities of everyday life; not only witnessing the evolution of the cities, but also playing an active role in such evolution. Having a descriptive nature, the study relies on narrative inquiry by adopting qualitative analysis. Polkinghorne's paradigmatic mode of analysis is adopted as the method for analysis of narratives. In doing so, the study examines the narrative data in order to reveal common themes or salient constructs and organize them under several categories. Consequently, findings would be arranged around descriptions of themes that are common across narratives.

***

"TURKISH COFFEE" AS A CULTURAL PRODUCT AND COMPETITIVE ANALYSIS FOR TURKISH COFFEE

Nevin Karabıyık Yerden, İlknur Ergün Tuncay

Abstract

In this study, it is aimed to investigate the competition analysis of Turkish coffee which is evaluated within the scope of culture product. It is revealed that Turkish Coffee, which Unesco has received on the list of "intangible cultural heritage" in 2013, is a cultural heritage on an international level and can be regarded as a cultural product. Cultural products are considered as an important competitive element that includes creative or artistic elements and contributes to the development of countries. In this sense, it is possible to say that cultural product contributes to social and economic development both nationally and internationally. In this study, competition analysis for Turkish coffee which is considered within the scope of culture product is examined on the basis of M. Porter's Five Forces Model. The five power models of M. Porter consist of the competitors in the sector, the threat of new entrepreneurs in the sector, the threat of substitute goods or services, the bargaining power of suppliers and the bargaining power of buyers. Turkish coffee is analyzed according to these Five Forces Model in the international area. This study is conceptual study based on literatüre review. Determination of the competitors of the Turkish coffee which is considered as a cultural product and the analysis of international competition in the field are examined.

***

FOODSCAPES AND PLACE-MAKING: QUESTIONS OF METHODOLOGY

Defne Karaosmanoğlu

Abstract

The global movements of food bring interesting, unexpected and peculiar stories. When the global cultural flows integrate with particular geographies and histories, they become "radically context dependent" (Appadurai, 1999: 47). Furthermore, food is not just a commodity, but a particular one, which has its own language of smell and taste. Therefore, foodscapes (Ferrero, 2002) as one of the scapes of global cultural flows (Appadurai, 1996), should include the global circulation of aromas and flavors. Food is a powerful agent of place-making and also place branding and to be able to study food and place, we should not neglect the senses. In this paper, my aim is not only to understand the role of foodscapes when dealing with place-making and branding, but also to find methodological ways to study the senses in that respect. This paper tries to answer the following questions: What is the role of foodscapes in place-making and how should we approach the global circulation of aromas and flavors? How should we (or can we) study the senses of taste and smell? In other words, how can we turn senses into knowledge? In this paper, I propose two methodological approaches to be able to do sensory research within the context of global cultural flows. First one is self-reflexivity, and the second one is radical contextualization. I elaborate those approaches by looking at the intersection of food, foodscapes and cities through diverse examples from around the globe.

References

Appadurai, A. 1996. *Modernity at Large: Cultural Dimensions of Globalization.* Minneapolis: University of Minnesota Press.

Appadurai, A. 1999. Globalization and Research Imagination. *International Social Science Journal* 2 (June): 229- 38.

Ferrero, S. 2002. *Comida sin par.* Consumption of Mexican Food in Los Angeles: "Foodscapes" in a Transnational Consumer Society. In *Food Nations: Selling Taste in Consumer Societies,* eds. Warren Belasco and Philip Scranton. New York: Routledge.

Lunch Break: Restaurant	Akdeniz	13.00- 14:30

SESSION 4 – Foodscapes and Tourism: Cases and Methodologies

Room: Nuri Özaltın Conference Hall
Chair: Beykan Çizel
14:30-16:00

Erkan Sezgin, Hediye Çetinkaya - DEVELOPING A SCALE TO IDENTIFY WORKING CONDITIONS AND MOTIVATORS OF FAST FOOD RESTAURANT EMPLOYEES

Hilal Erkuş Öztürk, Pieter Terhorst - STRATEGIES OF STANDARDIZATION AND DIFFERENTIATION OF RESTAURANTS IN A MASS-TOURISM CITY: THE CASE OF ANTALYA

Mert Uydacı, Nevin Karabıyık Yerden, Başak Değerli, İlknur Ergün Tuncay - EFFECTS ON EXPERIENCE VALUE OF AUGMENTED REALITY (AR) EXPERIENCE; A RESEARCH ON AR MENU APPLICATION

Oğuz Taşpınar - ANALYSIS OF TOURISM EDUCATION IN GASTRONOMY AND CULINARY ARTS DEPARTMENTS

Anna-Maria Saarela, Sari Jääskeläinen, Tarja Kupiainen, Päivi Mantere, Vappu Salo - INNOVATION ECOSYSTEM - FOOD CONNECTING PEOPLE AND CULTURES - DEVELOPING A NEW CO-CREATION MODEL WITH EDUCATION AND INDUSTRY

DEVELOPING A SCALE TO IDENTIFY WORKING CONDITIONS AND MOTIVATORS OF FAST FOOD RESTAURANT EMPLOYEES

Erkan Sezgin, Hediye Çetinkaya

Abstract

The motivation of the employees is an influencing success factor for the companies in all industries and service industries are not the exceptions. For service business, motivating employees is not that easy, though. Employees may experience underperformance sometimes even if they love their work. Such underperformance of employees may help working reluctantly, increasing stress, fearing of failure and sometimes even leaving job.

Fast food restaurants (FFRs) are time-competing and fast businesses not only for consumers but also for employees. In FFRs, where the average age of employees is lower than in other restaurants, managements concentrate on the methods for increasing their employees' work and workplace motivations. Some of these methods include frequent rises at work, different positions where rises are frequent, and prizes such as "employee of the month".

In this particular study, a scale was developed that aims to reveal the factors that increase and decrease the motivation of employees in FFRs as well as the conditions affect the employees at work. The total population is the employees at varied positions in FFRs. The sample of the study on the other hand, is 172 employees agreed to participate in the survey from various positions of Istanbul Burger King FFR branches in 2018 winter. Employing Exploratory Factor Analysis (EFA), three dimensions have emerged, namely 'workplace performance increasers', 'workplace performance reducers' and 'conditions affecting the employees'.

Confirmatory Factor Analysis (CFA) was also employed in the study to verify the scale which was finalised with 16-items and three-dimensions.

***

STRATEGIES OF STANDARDIZATION AND DIFFERENTIATION OF RESTAURANTS IN A MASS-TOURISM CITY: THE CASE OF ANTALYA

Hilal Erkuş Öztürk, Pieter Terhorst

Abstract

This paper is about strategies of standardization and differentiation of restaurants in a mass-tourism city of Antalya. The reason for having chosen restaurants as object of research is that, they are more differentiated than hotels and a few other tourism related sectors. Differentiations in the restaurant industry are the opposite of McDonaldization (rationalization). The main argument of this paper is that the restaurant market of Antalya is much more differentiated than expected such a mass tourism city. In the empirical research, we try to answer the following research questions.

- Are low-quality, standardized restaurants more oriented to the tourism market than higher quality, less standardized restaurants?

- Are higher-quality restaurants more differentiated with respect to new dishes and/or new services than lower-quality restaurants?

- Are restaurants predominantly visited by tourists less differentiated than restaurants predominantly visited by locals or visited by a mix of locals and tourists?

- Does the strategy restaurateurs follow depend on the specific urban sub-milieu in which they are located?

The empirical research is based on interviews with more than 50 managers and chefs of restaurants in Antalya. The empirical analysis is based on quantitative methods of relational analysis. The main finding is that restaurants of high quality, visited by a mix groups including locals and tourists, and are located in a specific urban milieu, are most differentiated.

***

EFFECTS ON EXPERIENCE VALUE OF AUGMENTED REALITY (AR) EXPERIENCE; A RESEARCH ON AR MENU APPLICATION

Mert Uydacı, Nevin Karabıyık Yerden, Başak Değerli, İlknur Ergün Tuncay

Abstract

The aim of this study is to investigate the effects of the experience of the restaurant consumer on the experience value with the application of a menu made with augmented reality (AR). The culinary culture of a region, such as a window for people to recognize other cultures. Gastronomy is an integral part of the tourism experience. In some cases, it may be the basic motivation for travel. Interactivity is becoming more and more important every day in terms of introducing culinary cultures, which have an important place in the experience of the city, to tourists in different forms. This research; In interactive AR application, what the consumer has done with the elements of this new communication environment, the experience of using the communication media in reaching the contents, satisfying the needs or getting some needs is important in terms of the influence of the experience value. In terms of experience values city experience will be very important in the destination marketing. In this research, it is requested that the restaurant consumer should respond to questionnaire after viewing the videos of an interactive menu application designed with AR. A Likert scale of 5 was used in the study. An online questionnaire was prepared for the study and easy sampling method was used. Research data is analyzed using factor analysis, regression analysis and other advanced statistical analysis techniques.

***

ANALYSIS OF TOURISM EDUCATION IN GASTRONOMY AND CULINARY ARTS DEPARTMENTS

Oğuz Taşpınar

Abstract

Although gastronomy is defined in lots of sources as science of eating-drinking, recently it gained popularity within tourism. Even though it is evaluated within limits of fine arts, geography and law in foreign literature, it is known as the "science of life" by researchers.

Gastronomy education is given in faculties of fine arts in Turkey for the first time. It will be right to see this situation as an aesthetic approach. Yet today, existing structural functioning of gastronomy does not highlight aesthetics and arts. According to 2018 data, number of universities which offers gastronomy education is reached to 38 in Turkey. Departments continue their education in tourism faculties. Despite adequate number of gastronomy education giving institutions, it is a question that those departments in tourism faculties are fully capable of giving tourism education as purposed. One of the most important points for researchers to pay attention about the subject is curriculum. It is expected from gastronomy, which is under the roof of tourism, to give education based on tourism. In other words, it is seen that most valid way for specialization of gastronomy students in their fields is tourism.

In this study, it is tried to give information about existing departments while focusing on what should be done about gastronomy education. Kind of the research is qualitative and content analysis is done while evaluating the data. Within entire catalogue of courses, it is observed that courses are mainly related with culinary professions and courses based on tourism are quite less. In this regard, it is thought that students of gastronomy and culinary will be working at tourism businesses with a low level tourism knowledge.

***

INNOVATION ECOSYSTEM - FOOD CONNECTING PEOPLE AND CULTURES - DEVELOPING A NEW CO-CREATION MODEL WITH EDUCATION AND INDUSTRY

Anna-Maria Saarela, Sari Jääskeläinen, Tarja Kupiainen, Päivi Mantere, Vappu Salo

Abstract

The Ministry of Education and Culture in Finland is funding a ReKey -project (2017-2019) for improving the education of tourism and hospitality at 13 universities of applied sciences in close collaboration with the industry. The aim of the project is to improve a novel co-creation model, which strengthens the role of universities of applied sciences in national and international innovation ecosystems.

Tourism and Hospitality industry and companies require novel information and solutions for creating business more profitable and attractive in continuous change of the working life. Therefore, knowledge transfer activities between all ecosystem partners are essential and crucial elements for successful growth and learning. Dynamic ecosystems include versatile partners from different levels and regions and allows several activities.

Food connecting people and cultures - innovation ecosystem will be piloted and created during the ReKey-project. The innovation ecosystem will be implemented in cooperation with food, culture and tourism partners regionally, nationally and internationally by multidisciplinary team.

Food connecting people and cultures - activities involve students, professors and food and tourism industry etc. into knowledge transfer activities in many ways. We can provide innovative teaching and learning activities on site at all school levels, universities, companies, such as food preparations sessions, courses, internships, visiting professors/experts, excursions, interactive workshops, seminars etc.

In a long run, the created ecosystem will enable and support the knowledge exchange of different food cultures, exchange of expertise, professional growth, improved employment, new product and service innovations, such as improved knowledge of novel ingredients/products, processing technologies as well as business contacts fastening import and export activities among entrepreneurs, research institutes, education and development organizations and students, especially from an international point of view. Creating an innovative ecosystem for food and tourism partners regionally, nationally and internationally, understanding consumer behavior is a key for financial and sustainable business success.

Gala Dinner – Venue: TBC   19:30

www.tastecity.net
www.tplondon.com
www.transnationalmarket.com

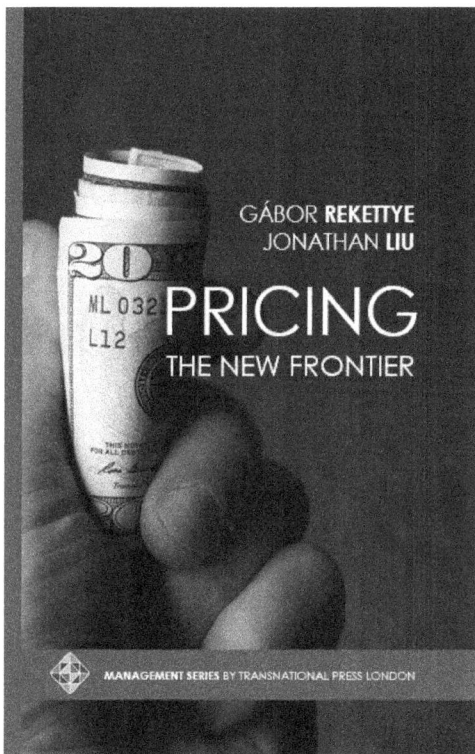

EXCHANGE RATE
VOLATILITY
IN EMERGING ECONOMIES

Abdulkader M. ALJANDALI

MANAGEMENT SERIES BY TRANSNATIONAL PRESS LONDON

IMAGE OF
ISTANBUL
IMPACT OF ECOC 2010 ON
THE CITY IMAGE
Evinç DOĞAN

MANAGEMENT SERIES BY TRANSNATIONAL PRESS LONDON

INTERNATIONAL
OPERATIONS, INNOVATION &
SUSTAINABILITY

Arvind Upadhyay
Celine Vadam
Vikas Kumar
Jose Arturo Garza-Reyes

MANAGEMENT SERIES BY TRANSNATIONAL PRESS LONDON

Presenters Index

www.ingramcontent.com/pod-product-compliance
Lightning Source LLC
Chambersburg PA
CBHW071122210326
41519CB00020B/6392